AGALLOCHA

The Tree of Life

by Warnette B. Patterson

Order this book online at www.trafford.com
or email orders@trafford.com

Most Trafford titles are also available at major online book retailers.

Note for Librarians: A cataloguing record for this book is available from Library
and Archives Canada at www.collectionscanada.ca/amicus/index-e.html

Printed in Victoria, BC, Canada.

ISBN: 978-1-4269-1565-9 (sc)

*Our mission is to efficiently provide the world's finest, most comprehensive book publishing
service, enabling every author to experience success. To find out how to publish your book, your
way, and have it available worldwide, visit us online at www.trafford.com*

Trafford rev. 10/16/2009

www.trafford.com

North America & international
toll-free: 1 888 232 4444 (USA & Canada)
phone: 250 383 6864 ♦ fax: 812 355 4082

For in Adam all die, even so in Christ shall all be made alive.

Warnette B. Patterson

Agallocha

TO GOD MY FATHER, JESUS, MY SAVIOUR AND THE HOLY GHOST, MY COMFORTER, BY WHOM I'M FILLED. WHAT A WONDERFUL THING IT IS TO HEAR YOUR VOICE, I THANK YOU FOR SPEAKING TO ME, as I believed and wrote: you spoke it. It is my prayer that every one who reads this book will be blessed and hear you speak also.

Dedicated to my family and friends presented to every believer to urge every sinner, to get saved and live, for real.

Notice

This book is intended to encourage life.

Warnette B. Patterson is neither a botanist horticulturist and possesses no degrees in the medical field; however the tree agallocha does exist. This book is intended to help you draw near to God and search out the word for yourself.

The scripture were written from the KJV bible.

"For the law of the spirit of life in Christ Jesus hath made me free from the law of sin and death. {Romans 8:2} I will ransom them from the power of the grave: I will redeem them from death: O death; I will be thy plagues; O grave, I will be thy destruction: repentance shall be hid from mine eyes. {Hosea 13:14} he that hath an ear, let him hear what the Spirit saith unto the churches: to him that overcometh will I give to eat of the Tree of Life, which is in the midst of the paradise of God. {Revelation 2:7}KJV

Preface

Now a thing was secretly brought to me, and mine ear received a little thereof.

In thoughts from the visions of the night, when deep sleep falleth on men. Fear came upon me, and trembling, which made all mine bones to shake.

Then a spirit passed before my face, the hair of my flesh stood up:

It stood still, but I could not discern the form thereof: and there was an image before my eyes, there was silence, and I heard a voice, saying, "Shall mortal man be more just than God? Shall a man be more pure than his maker?

They are destroyed from morning to evening: they perish for ever without any regarding it."(They are dying from lack of knowledge).

Thus saith the LORD, he that created the heavens, and stretched them out: he that spread forth the earth, and that which cometh out of it: he that giveth breath to the people upon it, and spirit to them that walk therein:

"I the LORD have called thee in righteousness, and will hold thine hand, and will keep thee, and give thee for a covenant of the people, for a light of the Gentiles.

To open the blind eyes, to bring out the prisoners from the prison, and them that sit in darkness out of the prison house.

I am the LORD: that is my name: and my glory will I not give to another, neither my praise to graven images.

Behold the former things are come to pass, and new things do I declare: before they spring forth I tell you of them.

Surely the LORD GOD will do nothing, but he revealeth his secret unto his servants the prophets. I have declared the former things from the beginning: and they went forth out of my mouth and I shewed them; I did them suddenly, and they came to pass.

Remember the former things of old; For I am God, and there is none else: I am God, and there is none like me.

Declaring the end from the beginning, and from ancient times the things are not yet done, saying my counsel shall stand: and I will do all my pleasure:

Calling a ravenous bird from the east, the man that executeth my counsel from a far country: yea, I have purposed it, I will do it".

Chapter 1

T hus saith the LORD, the Holy One of Israel, and his maker, "Ask me things to come concerning my sons, and concerning the works of my hands, command ye me.

I have made the earth, and created man upon it: I even I my hands have stretched out the heavens, and all their hosts have I commanded.

I have raised him up in righteousness, and I will direct all his ways: he shall build my city, and he shall let go my captives not for price nor reward, saith the LORD OF hosts.

I have even from the beginning declared it to thee; before it came to pass I shewed it thee: lest they should say, mine idol hath done them: and my graven image, and my molten image, hath commanded them.

Thou hast heard, see all this; and will not ye declare it? I have shewed thee, new things from this time, even hidden things, and thou didst not know them". AGALLOCHA is what I heard, a simple word: AGALLOCHA.

When I thought to know this; it was too painful for me; until I went into the sanctuary of God: then understood I the end.

This is what the Holy Spirit caused me to understand.

The LORD said, "For I know the thoughts that I think toward you, saith the LORD, thoughts of peace and not evil, to give you an expected end."

The purpose of the law is to make you understand the holiness of God's character.

It set boundaries between God and you, as the offenders of his law. It was established to let us know what sins are, and it clearly explain the penalty of committing them, making us aware of what not do, but it wasn't designed to give us power to reframe from committing sins, and therefore we must pay the penalty of death for committing sin. Because death is the payment for sin.

The Bible says that when sin is finished it bringeth forth death. But the gift of God is eternal life through Jesus Christ our Lord.

Jesus came to show us the Father's will; his divine plans for our lives, by performing the Kingdom of God through example: He healed the sick, he cleansed the leapers, and he raised the dead, and cast out devils. He sealed God the Father's will for our lives; to restoration: with his own blood, by his death burial and resurrection, by way of the cross.

And as if that wasn't enough, he sent us the Holy Ghost, our Comforter to be received by us, to remain in us, operating in our lives to reveal the truth to us; because he is the Spirit of truth.

The Spirit of Truth, is with us to sift out all lies that comes from the wicked on; and he provides the power and the will, for us to reframe from sin.

His strength gives us the power to perform the works of God in our lives for others.

The Holy Spirit brings life with him, and power to change our character into the image of God by his Spirit.

He (JESUS) said, "We will come in and make our abode. He said, if a man love me, he will keep my words: and my Father will love him, and he will come to him, and make our abode with him.

Believe me that I am in the Father, and the Father in me: or else believe me for the very words sake.

Verily, Verily, I say unto you, he that believeth on me, the works I do he shall do also; and greater works than these he shall do; because I go unto my Father.

Jesus said,

"And whatsoever ye shall ask in my name, that will I do, that the Father may be glorified in the Son.

If ye shall ask anything in my name, I will do it.

If ye love me keep my commandments, And I will pray the Father, and he shall give you another Comforter, that he may abide with you forever, Even the Spirit of truth, whom the world cannot receive, because it seeth him not, neither knoweth him: but ye know him; for he dwelleth in you, and shall be in you.

But the Comforter, which is the Holy Ghost, whom the Father will send in my name, he shall teach you all things, and bring all things to your remembrance, whatsoever I have said."

The first thing that the Holy Spirit wants to teach us is: the precepts of God.

Precepts; are the rules and principles of God. The way the word of God is set up in the Bible, and He leads and guides us through the truth. The precepts are to help us to understand the holiness and righteousness of God's character, it lets us know most assuredly that God's Spirit dwells in all of God's believers.

The manifestation of his Spirit in us is the fruit of the Spirit, which is, love, joy, peace, longsuffering, gentleness, goodness, faith, meekness, and temperance, against which there is no law.

The Holy Spirit abides in us to give us strength to continue on, as he help us understand and receive the truth about God the Father, and the loving relationship that he have with his Son Jesus, and their unity with the Holy Ghost.

He teaches us that as heirs we are joint heirs of Christ therefore sons of God by adoption.

He causes us to understand by the conviction of our sin, and instructions, by the Word of God. He the Holy Spirit will only say what he hears the Father say, and he shows us what Jesus want to make known to us, by his Spirit, even hands on examples.

He is the power behind God's Word to bring it to past, just as he is the power behind our words, to bring them to past.

The Holy Spirit assures us that we are not forgotten: "For I **know** the thoughts that I think toward you," saith the LORD, "Thoughts of peace and not evil, to give you and expected end." (Not of death, but of life.)

"Then shall you call upon me, and ye shall go and pray unto me, and I will hearken unto you. And ye shall seek me, and find me, when ye shall search for me for me with all your heart."

Then I heard; "AGALLOCHA; Behold I will bring it health and cure, and I will cure them, and will reveal unto them the abundance of peace and truth.

And I will cause the captivity of Judah and the captivity of Israel to return and will build them, as at the first.

And I will cleanse them from all their iniquities, whereby they have transgressed against me. And it shall be to me a name of joy. A praise and an honour before all the nations of the earth, which shall hear all the good that I do unto them: and they shall fear and tremble for all the goodness and for all the prosperity that I procure unto it."

He has said, which heard the words of God, which saw the visions of the Almighty falling into a trance, but having his eyes open:
"How goodly are your tents, O, Jacob, and thy tabernacles, O Israel!
As the valleys are they spread forth, as gardens by the river's side, as the trees of lign aloes (AGALLOCHA), which the LORD hath planted, and cedar trees besides the waters,".
When I thought to know this it was too painful for me: AGALLOCHA.

The Bible says,
But now is made manifest by the appearing of our Saviour Jesus Christ, who hath abolished death and hath brought life and immortality to light through the gospel. 1 TIMOTHY 1:10

Chapter 2

Thus saith the LORD GOD, "Behold, O my people, I will open your graves, and cause you to come out of your graves, and bring you into the land of Israel.

And ye shall know that I am the LORD, when I have opened your graves, O my people, and brought you up out of your graves.

And shall put my Spirit in you, and ye shall live, and I shall place you in your own land; then shall you know that I the LORD have spoken it, and will perform it," saith the LORD. **"AGALLOCHA?"**

(As sinners we offend the holiness of God's image, which is a moral evil, and when we do commit a moral evil against God, it becomes a crime (sin), punishable by death, because it is a sin.

We have been given a dispensation. A dispensation is; a period of time under which all man kind is answerable to God for how they have heard and obeyed the revelation of the gospel of Jesus Christ, and of salvation received in the allotted time.

This dispensation is how we have heard and believed the gospel and have applied it to our lives, daily.

God our Father, having predestinated us into the adoption as his children by Jesus Christ to himself, according to the good pleasure of his will.)

To the praise and the glory of his grace, wherein he has made us acceptable in the beloved. In whom we have redemption through his blood, the forgiveness of sin, according to the riches of his grace; Wherein he hath abounded toward us in all wisdom and prudence;

Having made known unto us the mystery of his will, according to his good pleasure, which he hath purposed in himself;

That in the dispensation of the fullness of times, he might gather together in one all things in Christ, both which are in heaven, and which are on earth: even in it.

In whom we have obtained an inheritance, being predestinated according to the purpose of him who worketh all things after the counsel of his own will: that we should be to the praise of his glory, whom first trusted in Christ.

In whom ye also trusted, after that ye heard the word of truth, the gospel of your salvation, in whom also, ye were sealed with the Holy Spirit of promise.

Chapter 3

And after these things I saw four angles standing on the four corners of the earth, holding the four winds of the earth, that the wind should not blow on the earth, nor on the sea, nor on any tree.

And I saw another angel ascending from the east, having the seal of the living God (this seal of the living God is the seal of the Holy Ghost that is placed in our foreheads, which identify us as children of God) and he cried with a loud voice to the four angels, to whom it was given to hurt the earth and the sea.

AND the fifth angel sounded, and I saw a star fall from heaven: and to him was given the key of the bottomless pit; and there arouse a smoke out of the bottomless pit: as the smoke of a great furnace; and the sun and the air was darkened by reason of the smoke of the pit.

And there came out of the smoke locusts upon the earth: and unto them was given power as the scorpions of the earth have power.

And it was commanded them that they should not hurt the grass of the earth, neither any green thing, neither any tree; but only those men which have not the seal of God in their foreheads.

HE cried also in my ears with a loud voice, saying, "Cause them that have the charge over the city to draw near, even every man with a destroying weapon in his hand."

And behold, six men came from the way of the higher gate, which lieth toward the north, and every man a slaughter weapon in his hand; and one man among them was clothed in linen, with a writer's inkhorn by his side: and he went in, and stood besides the brazen alter.

And the glory of the God of Israel was gone up from the cherub, whereupon he was, to the threshold of the house. And he called to the man clothed with linen, which had the writer's inkhorn by his side:

And the LORD said unto him, "Go through the midst of the city, through the midst of Jerusalem, and set a mark upon the foreheads of the men that sigh and that cry for all the abomination that be done in the midst thereof."

And to the others he said in mine hearing, "Go ye after him through the city, and smite: let not your eye spare, neither have ye pity;
Slay utterly old and young, both maids and little children, and women: but come not near any man upon whom is the mark (The mark of the Holy Ghost) and begin at my sanctuary."

Then they began at the ancient men which were before the house.
And he said unto them, "Defile the house, and fill the courts with the slain: go forth." And they went forth, and slew in the city.

And it came to pass, while he was slaying them, and I was left, that I fell upon my face, and cried, and said, "Ah, Lord GOD! Wilt thou destroy all the residue of Israel in the pouring out of thy fury upon Jerusalem?"

Then said he unto me, "The iniquity of the house of Israel is exceeding great, and the land is full of blood, and the city full of perverseness: for they say, The LORD has forsaken the earth, and the earth seeth not."

And as for me also, mine eye shall not spare, neither will I have pity, but will recompence their way upon their heads."

And behold, the man clothed , which had the inkhorn by his side, reported the matter; saying, "I have done as thou hast commanded me." **Ezekiel 9:1-11**.

Chapter 4

T
he Bible says: For if ye live after the flesh, ye shall die: but if ye through the Spirit do mortify the deeds of the body, ye shall live,

For as many as are led by the Spirit of God, they are the sons of God.

But if the Spirit of him that raised up Jesus from the dead dwell in you he that raised up Christ from the dead shall also quicken your mortal bodies(keep you alive also.) by his Spirit that dwelleth in you.

Which is the earnest of our inheritance until the redemption of the purchased possession, unto the praise of his glory?

For God hath not given us the spirit of fear: but of power and of love, and of a sound mind. (God has restored us with his Spirit that of which Satan had caused to depart from Adam and Eve, and us.)

Who hath saved us and called us with a holy calling, not according our works but according to his own purpose and grace, which was given us in Christ before the world began.

Buy is now made manifest, by the appearing of our Saviour Jesus Christ, who hath abolished death, and hath brought life and immortality to light through the gospel: (As it was stated before).

And your covenant with death shall be disannulled and your agreement with hell shall not stand.

Jesus said: "Fear not; I am the first and the last: I am he that liveth; and was dead; and, behold, I am alive for evermore Amen; and have the keys of hell and death.

Write these things which thou hast seen, and the things which are and things which shall be hereafter.

It is the Spirit that quickeneth the flesh profiteth nothing, the words that I speak unto you, they are Spirit and they are life.

Now the just shall live by faith: but if any man draw back, my soul shall have no pleasure in him.

But without faith it is impossible to please him, for he that cometh to God must believe that he is, and that he is a rewarder of them that diligently seek him.

Now faith is the substance of things hoped for and the evidence of things not seen". (When you have faith in God, it is able to hold you. You are able to trust him and hold on to the preordained promises of God, with confidence in his word, that he love you enough not to go back on his promises.

When we have confidence in God it allows his love to be released in us.

To allow you to be compassionate enough to resolve an impossible problem for yourself or others, with confidence of the love of God.

That the love of God toward his children can manifest a change.

Knowing that without doubt "it" what ever you speak, will come to pass.

Therefore, even though you must wait on its manifestation, but even in your waiting you will not suffer anxiety, because you are waiting with hope, and hope will not allow you to be ashamed of God, because we have confidence in him.

Therefore, because you are steadfast and unmovable, it causes action to be taken by God to bring a desired resolution to pass, concerning a promise that God has made to us in his spoken word or that you have spoken, even to solve an impossible problem for yourself or for others.

You have been chosen by God, for public display, to a position that you should be ready to defend with all obedience.

You will become the vessel that is able to do something for someone that they are not able to do for themselves, even where there seems to be no other solution.

You should be able to receive, and respond to the love of God, (Taking action for that person, when directed by the Holy Spirit.) to release the love of God into someone's life, believing that God is and that he is a rewarder of those that diligently seek him.

He is able to do exceeding abundantly and above all that we can think or imagine.

That is what sets love free to move faith to perform the expected, and bring the favored desire to past.

So then faith cometh by hearing, and hearing by the word of God.

Have faith in God-God is love. Everyone that has faith in him is entitled to that resource of love.

Faith works by love. Your output of that of love lends passion to be bestowed on others. It makes them receptors of the resource of love that God has stored in you.

Your output of that resource of love is to: pronounce the right of a matter that needs a resolution to be resolved and to bind or loose on earth when it is an impossible problem for us to resolve.

To pronounce- is to speak the right of a matter to be dissolved, having the power to influence the favorable outcome, of a desired resolution.

You have this power working in you to influence relief with the manifestation of a cure, to command the devils seize to end, (he is not a friend but the enemy,) to loose the captives that they may go free to receive healing in Jesus' name.

The Bible says: "But we have this treasure in earthern vessels, that the Excellency of the power may be of God, and not of us.

Now unto him that is able to exceeding abundantly above all that we ask or think, according to the power that worketh in us". (You are able to inject the cure, even to life itself.)

Chapter 5

"Give ear, O my people, to my law: incline your ease to the words of my mouth.

I will open my mouth in a parable: I will utter dark sayings of old."

This prophesy of parables was fulfilled in Jesus, saying: "I will open my mouth in parables; I will utter things which have been kept secret from the foundation of the world."

He answered and said, "Because it is given to you to know the mysteries of the kingdom of heaven, but to them it is not given.

Blessed are the eyes which see the things that you see. For I tell you, that many prophets and kings have desired to see those things which ye see, and have not seen them; and to hear those things and have not heard them.

For this people's heart is waxed gross and their ears are dull of hearing: and their eyes they have closed: lest at any time they should see with their eyes, and hear with their ears, and understand with their heart, and should be converted and I should heal them.

But blessed are your eyes, for they see: and your ears, for they hear".

(Our temples were set for demolition, but now they can be restored to the original state as intended by God.)

And he spake a parable unto them: "No man putteth a piece of a new garment upon an old: if otherwise, then both the new maketh a rent and the piece that was taken out of the new, agreeth not with the old.

And no man putteth new wine into old bottles; else the new wine will burst the bottles, and be spilled, and the bottles shall perish.

New wine must be put into new bottles; and both are preserved.

No man having drunk old wine straight way desireth new; for he sayest the old is better." Mark 2: 22-23 explains it like this: No man also seweth a piece of new cloth on an old garment: else the new piece that fill it up, taketh away from the old, and the rent is made worse.

And no man putteth new wine into old bottles, else the new wine doeth burst the bottles, and the wine is spilled, and the bottles will be marred; but new wine is put into new bottles.

The old garment that could not receive the new wine, (dispensation) is because it became stressed from the lack of insight, and strength, and was not able to be strengthened, because of the dullness of hearing.

The new piece of cloth that was added to the old was more vibrant in color, and detail, it was strong, but the stress of the old, caused the old to become faded and worn, dull and weak.

The stress of the old wine skins, and the old garment, could not accept the new dispensation, of the revelation of the gospel of Jesus Christ, that he is in very deed the Son of the Living God.

The strict adherence of the law kept them bound, So much so that they refused to be strengthened, made new, to be born again, and complete: by the Holy Ghost, because they refused to accept Jesus as Saviour and LORD the Son of God; even also as many none believers today.

Jesus came with open public display; through demonstration of the power glory and the love of God, he was moved with compassion.

He clearly showed that he is the Son of God with grace and mercy filled with love and truth.

Chapter 6

T he purpose of the Law is to make us understand the holiness of God's character, in all his righteousness. Because when God made us he made us in his image. Jesus showed us what that image is to look like.

Our boundaries were clearly set, but, there was a act of disobedience that caused man to cross over into forbidden territory and partaking of the fruit that God had commanded them not to eat thereof.

They did eat of the tree of good and evil, and their character was changed, they became afraid, and ashamed, and they tried to cover themselves. The tree that they did eat from caused fear, sickness and death, and it came as a result of sin, through disobedience.

The same three things that the devil talked to Eve about that caused her to eat from the tree of good and evil is the same three things that the devil tried to get Jesus to do.

The bible says,

THEN was Jesus led up of the Spirit into the wilderness to be tempted of the devil.

And when he had fasted forty days and forty nights, he was afterwards hungered.

And when the tempter came to him, he said," If thou be the Son of God, command that these stones (these diamonds, rubies, onyx, sapphire, emerald, jasper, gold and so on) be made bread."

But he answered and said, "It is written, Man shall not live by bread alone, but by every word that proceedeth out of the mouth of God."

Then the devil taketh him up into the holy city, and setteth him on a pinnacle of the temple,

And he saith to him, If thou be the Son of God, cast thyself down: for it is written, He shall give his angels charge concerning thee: and in their hands they shall bear thee up, lest at any time thou dash thy foot against a stone.

Jesus said unto him, "It is written again, Thou shalt not tempt the Lord thy God."(Why should Jesus the Son of the Living God try to prove any thing to the devil, God said it and Jesus did not doubt that God would do as he said, Jesus has complete confidence in God: when God says it, 'it" is.)

Again, the devil taketh him up into an exceeding high mountain, and sheweth him the kingdoms of the world, and the glory of them:

And saith unto him, "All these things will I give thee, if thou wilt fall down and worship me.")

The Bible says, In the beginning was the Word (Jesus), and the Word (Jesus) was with God, and the Word was God (Jesus). (As the Son of God he had also the power of God, therefore being equal to God). The same was in the beginning with God (JEHOVAH).

All things were made by him; and without him was not any thing made that was made.

In him was life; and the life was the light of men.

Now I say to you; how does the devil think that he can give Jesus something that even he doesn't own. But to go to the owner and maker of all things, and try to persuade him that it belongs to him; is something else.

But the devil does that very thing to us. He tries to trade your life; that what is rightfully your, for something that he know is lifeless, for just one act of worship toward him.

Then saith Jesus unto him, "Get thee hence, Satan: for it is written, Thou shalt worship the Lord thy God, and him only shalt thou serve."

Then the devil leaveth him, and angels came and ministered unto him.

Just as Eve was hungry, Jesus fasted for forty days and forty nights (he was also hungry), and he also was tempted by the devil. The devil wanted Jesus to change God's order by making the stones bread.

Jesus can make stones bread but that is not God's order.

He persuaded Eve to eat the forbidden fruit that could not reproduce but only kill. But he could not persuade Jesus to change the course of it.

It was not how redemption is planned.

But even then Jesus secured salvation for man He over came the devil and made a way of restoration for all that would call upon his name.

Jesus presented us with the call, just as he did the chosen disciples; and that is to be the results of the power of God in time, by the Holy Spirit, to bring the kingdom of God into view.

Therefore you are a chosen vessel that has an indwelling, of the divine unlimited source of Gods' power, ready to be revealed; to carry out our Father's will.

The new dispensation of new vessels and being instructed not to put new cloth on old tear, on old garments is because the character of the old garment has become weak and warn, it has lost its brightness, the brilliance, the color, and most of the details have been faded and lost.

The reason that it is useless to put the new on the old, is because there will be no agreement in details, the wear and tear of the old garment, and the weakness of threads, just cannot hold on to the new threads, to hold on to the old is simply a waste of time, because the old won't be strengthened by the new.

The old will tear will worsen when, pressure is applied to it, and the separation of parts are imminent.

Neither do men put new wine in old wine skins, because it will tear and the wine be spilled. But if we put new wine in new bottles or wine skins, both will be preserve.

New wine skins or new bottles are more acceptable to the contents that are put in them, able and ready to receive change. The old garments or old wine skins are without the influence of the Holy Ghost, and will not change.

This new wine is influenced by the Holy Spirit of God, in all of his splender, glory, mercy, and power, aged to perfection, filled with the knowledge and promises of God, for you to be a blessing, with all confidence in the love of God, waiting to please God.

Without confidence, without faith in God, it is impossible to please him: your lack of trust, shows God that you are not, nor can you be content with him and his way, because you do mistrust his judgment and directions.

We will not find enjoyment, pleasure, nor can we be completely committed to love, trust and serve God the way we should.

Our distrust and none commitment to him, will not allow us to be satisfied with his plan for our lives, to come into covenant agreement of the Atonement to be fully committed to the glorified plan, and ask the Holy Spirit to lead and guide us into all truth, so that we may understand that we have been redeemed from the hands of the enemy and we are free to go, to live our lives free from sin and death.

Because of our sinful mistrusting nature, we believe that God is still planning our rescue. It is finished! It is finished! Let me repeat that phrase: IT IS FINISHED! Maybe one more time: IT IS FINISHED!!

Jesus is the door and the door remains open to everlasting life. Jesus said, "I am he that liveth and was dead and, behold, I am alive forevermore, Amen, and have the keys of hell and death."

He has unlocked the door and has taken the keys with him into heaven.

And mankind is still being bound with the old wine skins, and the tricks of the devil.

We are living like domesticated birds, God have given them unlimited skies to spread their wings and fly in, yet when they are captured by man, they become accustomed to their surroundings.

They are bound from freedom, put in cages, for man's enjoyment.

After this bird is trained for his cage, he will never stops preparing his wings for flight, yet when he is startled by sudden noise, or threatened by certain animals he will return to his cage, because it has become a safe haven for him, yet he continues to take care of his wings and feathers. He cannot conceive that he will never fly the blue skies, stretching his wings, and soaring as God has intended for him to do.

Although the bird has been captured he continues to prepare his feathers for flight, always hoping to use them as God has intended him to do.

JESUS opened the door and has given us divine protection, by his power, to defeat the enemy and to cast down every imagination that tries to exalt itself against the knowledge of God.

The Bible says that the last enemy of God, which is death. Jesus himself will destroy. Death is not Gods friend to get you to himself.

Hell is death's destination and the grave will follow him there. It was made for Satan and his angels, and enlarged for man because of man's own wickedness.

Let me say that again, "Death is not God's friend to get you to him."

1Corinthians 15: 20-26 reads:
But now is Christ risen from the dead, and become the first fruits of them that slept.

For since by man came death, by man came also the resurrection from the dead.
For as in Adam all die, even so in Christ shall all be made alive.
But everyone in his own order: Christ the first fruits; afterward they that are Christ's at his coming.
Then cometh the end, when we shall have delivered up the kingdom of God, even the Father: when he shall have put down all rule and authority and power.
For he must reign, till he hath put all enemies under his feet.

The last enemy that shall be destroyed is death.
And as we have borne the image of the earthly, we shall also bear the image of the heavenly,
For this corruption (sin) must put on incorruption (righteousness), and this mortal (human mind must be renewed to think like godly) must put on immortality (the mind of Christ to renew it self to love and live in eternity).

So, when this corruption(sinful nature) shall have put on incorruption(righteousness), and this mortal (and this dead way of thinking is done away with) shall have put on immortality (when we are able to accept the fact that Jesus paid the total cost for our sin and we are renewed in the Spirit of Christ), then shall be brought to pass the saying that is written,

Death is swallowed up in victory, O death, where is thy sting? O grave, where is thy victory?

The sting of death is sin, and the strength of sin is the law. For until the law was sin in the world; but sin is no more imputed where there is no law: (you don't need a law if you: are His, You will have no other God before him, You will put away from you every idol and all images, or any likeness of any thing that is in heaven, or the earth beneath, even in the water under the earth. You will not bow down nor serve them, for Jehovah is the Lord your God, and he is a jealous God. You will not take the name of the Lord thy God in vain. You will remember the Sabbath day, and keep it holy. You will honour your father and your mother: that your days may be long upon the land which the Lord thy God giveth thee. You will not kill. You will not commit adultery. You will not steal. You will not bear false witness against your neighbor.) against these there is no law.

Nevertheless death reigned from Adam to Moses, even over them that had not sinned after the similitude of Adam's transgression, who is a figure to come,

But not as the offence, so is the free gift, for if through the offence of one many be dead. Much more of the grace of God, and the gift by grace, which is by one man, Jesus Christ, hath abounded unto many.

And not as it was by one who sinned, so is the free gift: for the judgment was by one to condemnation, but this free gift is of many offenses unto justification,

For if by one man's offense death reigned by one much more they which receive abundance of grace of the gift of righteousness shall reign in life by one, Jesus Christ.

Therefore by one offense of one judgment came upon all men to condemnation: even so by the righteousness of the one free gift came upon all men unto justification of life. Proverbs 12:28 reads.

In the way of righteousness is life; and in the pathway thereof there is no death.

For as one man's disobedience many were made sinners, so by the obedience of one shall many be made righteous.

Moreover as sin hath reigned unto death, even so might grace reign through righteousness unto eternal life by Jesus Christ. (ETERNAL-without interruption or end-forever) Where sin abounded grace did much more abound.

Know ye not, that so many of us as were baptized unto Jesus Christ were baptized into his death?

Therefore we are buried with him by baptism into death: that like as Christ was raised up from the dead by glory of the Father, even so we also should walk in the newness of life.

For if we have been planted together in the likeliness of his death, we shall be also in the likeliness of his resurrection.

Knowing this, that our old man is crucified with him, that the body of sin might be destroyed, that henceforth we should not serve sin.

For ye are dead and your life is hid in with Christ in God.

For he that is dead is freed from sin: Now if we be dead with Christ, we believe that we shall also reign with him:

Knowing that Christ being raised from the dead dieth no more; death hath no more dominion over him.

For in that he died, he died unto sin once: but in that he liveth, he liveth unto God.

Likewise reckon ye also yourselves be dead indeed unto sin, but alive unto God through Jesus Christ our Lord.

So what does Agallocha have to do with mortal man's immortality? And what is Agallocha?

Chapter 7

J ust before we expose Agallocha, we must, accept the fact that we were created in the image of God.

(Image- a reproduction of the likeness of form of something or someone, in our case, we were created in the image of God.)

We were made in God's image, but changed into a lesser image, but now we are ready and willing to be restored back into the image of our Creator, God.

The conversion happened in the Garden of Eden.

The Bible says that we are made in his image, but sin entered in and our image changed.

As sinners, we offended the holiness of God's character, which is a moral evil. When you commit a moral evil against God, it becomes a crime, a sin, that punishable by death.

But, there is a dispensation given in the book of Genesis the second chapter, the fifteenth through the seventeenth verse and it reads:

And the Lord God commanded the man, saying, "of every tree of the garden thou mayest freely eat:

But the tree of the knowledge of good and evil, thou shalt not eat it: for in the day that thou eatest thereof, thou shalt surely die."

When man was created from the earth, God gave him a dispensation, a God given order not to eat of the tree of knowledge of good and evil.(God told him exactly what would happen if he did.)

And God said, Let us make man in our image: and let them have dominion over the fish of the sea, and over all the earth, and over every creeping thing that creepeth upon the earth: So God created man in his own image in the image of God created he him; male and female, created he them, and God said unto them be fruitful, and multiply and replenish the earth, and subdue it. (gain by it.) and have dominion over the fish of the sea, and the fowl of the air, and over every living thing that moveth upon the earth.

(And as God rules all things, he gave man dominion and ruler ship in the earth and over all that he had created on earth.)

And God said, "Behold, I have given you every herb bearing seed, which is upon the face of all the earth, and every tree in the which is fruit of a tree yielding seed: to you it shall be for meat.

And every beast of the earth, and every fowl of the air, and every thing that creepeth upon the earth, wherein there is life, I have given every green herb for meat:" and it was so.

And God saw everything that he had made and behold, it was very good.

And the evening and the morning were the fifth day.
Everything that God made, he looked at it himself and saw that it was very good.

And so it was that. All that God made was brought to perfection in six days.
And so God rested.

And out of the ground made the Lord God to grow every tree that is pleasant to the sight, and good for food: The tree of life also in the midst of the garden, and the tree of knowledge of good and evil.

Now the serpent was more subtle than any beast of the field which the Lord God had made.

And he said unto the woman, "Yea hath God said
ye shall not eat of the tree of the garden?" And the woman said unto the serpent, "We may eat of the fruit of the tree of the garden, but of the fruit of the tree which is in the midst of the garden
God hath said, "Ye shall not eat of it; neither shall ye touch it, lest ye die."

And the serpent said unto the woman, "Ye shall not surely die. For God doeth know that in the day ye eat thereof, then your eyes shall be opened, and ye shall be as gods, knowing good and evil."

(When the devil told Eve that she would not surely die, I can see a vision of him being kicked out of heaven and there he was among God's creation, on earth; but able to travel back and forth to God.
So when he told Eve that she would not surely die, he did not surely grasp God's power.

Just because he had already sinned and exalted himself, and was still able to have some power, he was able to still come to earth and still return to heaven and stand before God. He might have thought that Adam and Eve would be as he was.
But it is certain that he wanted dominion over God's creation, earth.)

Job 1:6-12,proves his ability to still stand before God. The bible says.
Now there was a day when the sons of God came and presented themselves before the Lord, and Satan came also among them.

And the Lord said unto Satan, "Has thou considered my servant Job, that there is none like him in the earth, a perfect and an upright man, one that feareth God, and executeth evil?"

Then Satan answered the Lord, and said, "Doeth Job fear God for nought? Has thou not made an hedge about him, and about his house, and about all that he hath on every side? Thou hast blessed the work of his hand, and the substance is increased in the land.

But put forth thine hand now, and touch all that he hath, and he will curse thee to thy face."

And the Lord said unto Satan, "Behold, all that he has is in thy power; only upon himself put not forth thine hand."

So Satan went forth from the presence of the Lord. (he tested Job, but Job withstood him) Satan came from eternity into time.

In eternity with God there is no death, no sickness and no poverty.

(In the beginning when Satan came to Eve about the tree of knowledge of good and evil he did not know death, as he didn't know the curse that God put in the tree.

The curse represented all that Satan is, sin, shame, fear, ambition, disobedience, and death.

Satan is a deceiver and a liar. He is a thief and a murderer.)

And the Bible says,

And when the woman saw that the tree was good for food and that it was pleasant to the eyes, and a tree to be desired to make one wise, she took of the fruit thereof, and did eat and gave also unto her husband with her: and he did eat.

(The knowledge that was received reversed man's ability to progress. Instead of the abundant life that God had planned for them, to be obedient, subdue, multiply, replenish, and be fruitful. God still wants us to gain, to increase, not decrease, the plan of God still holds fast today. But man is still decreasing.

So the man and woman did eat of the fruit from the tree of the knowledge of good and evil, the tree that did not have a seed initially to reproduce itself.

God gave power to Adam and Eve to rule on earth. He wanted man to walk in his image and to have his likeliness.

But Satan tried to take it from man for himself and for awhile he did.

He cannot reproduce he can only corrupt that what has already been created, and it is us that allow him to do so. But all that follow him will be destroyed by God).

Eve didn't realize that she was made in the image of God, after his likeliness. She didn't realize that the devil was about to deceive her by convincing her to disobey God.

He made it seem as though she would become even greater than she was. The reality of the deception was that her image became lesser and contrary to the image of God.

The Bible says,

And when the woman saw that the tree was good for food, and it was pleasant to the eyes, and a tree to make one wise, she took of the fruit thereof and did eat, and gave also unto her husband with her: and he did eat. And the eyes of them baths were opened, and they knew that they were naked: and they sewed fig leaves together, and made themselves aprons.

As soon as Adam and Eve did eat from the tree of the knowledge of good and evil, they converted, they under went a change.

Their natural beauty was abated. How they looked at each other was so different than when God had joined them together.

The Bible says, and they both were naked, the man and his wife, and were not ashamed of each other.

They were not ashamed.

After they ate of that tree of the knowledge of good and evil.

They were so moved by the knowledge of that they had received, that they made a false covering for themselves, false security false covering to hide their shame.

A fig leaf covering, something that would soon wither and crumble. The Bible says.

They heard the voice of the Lord God walking in the garden in the cool of the day. Adam and his wife hid themselves from the presence of the Lord God amongst the trees of the garden.

(They heard the voice of God uncontainable)

No longer could they feel the bond of relationship, between themselves and God.

The uniting bond that kept them in relationship had been so severally damaged between them, that they were in fear; and rightly so.

And the Bible says that Adam said, "I heard thy voice in the garden, and I was afraid because I was naked and I hid myself."

During the time that the Lord God was with Adam he brought to him his living creations and Adam named them all.

During to fall upon him, removing his rib, bringing forth the woman whom, Adam would name Eve, he was not troubled nor was he afraid.

When God commanded that he, not eat of the tree of the knowledge and of good and evil, Adam was not afraid.

But as soon as he had eaten of that tree, that he was commanded not to eat from, his eyes were opened.

The eyes of Adam were enlightened to evil, but without the courage or the ability or power to resist the change, and he and Eve were afraid and ashamed.

They had disobeyed a direct command from God, and something terrible had happened to them.

And they allowed fear to keep them from calling out to God, and asking for forgiveness, saying,   "Lord we have disobeyed you and now we are suffering for it. Lord God we are so sorry. Please forgive us. Will you please fix what we have broken?"

But they didn't go to God. Instead, God called out unto them asking, "Where art thou?
Who told thee that thou were naked? Hast thou eatest of the tree whereof I commanded thee that thou shouldest not eat?"
(This was the perfect opportunity for Adam to ask the Lord God for forgiveness for himself and Eve also, but he didn't seize the moment.)

The man said, "The woman whom thou gavest to be with me, she gave me of the tree and I did eat."

He covered the sin by telling the Lord God where he got the fruit from.

Proverbs 28:13 reads.
"He that covereth his sins shall not prosper: but whosoever confesseth and forsake them shall have mercy."
(What Adam said was not a confession of sin, but a covering of his sin.)

And the Lord God said unto the woman, "What is it that thou hast done?"
And the woman said, "The serpent beguiled me, and I did eat."

Satan saw God's creation, and from the beginning; he purposed to steal it from man, by allurement, the enticement of the fruit, because to look at it, it was desirable to the eye, and desirable to eat as food. If you ate it, it would make you wise.

It would make known the knowledge of itself. Of what was good and evil. And the results of what was received caused certain death, without their ability to reverse the curse.

So the lineage of God, his likeliness, natural beauty, ability to walk in God's power, under his covering, and the deeds of the earth all transferred to Satan, in one conversation with the serpent.

Adam and Eve had power over the devil, however they traded the power and dominion of earth for the lesser image of sin, shame, disobedience, and even death, Because they received the lying spirit..

Now because they acted on what they saw and heard and the desire of it, after the consumption of the fruit, immediately, their character changed.

Their reputation was destroyed because they were disobedient to God.

And what the Lord God had purposed for man on earth had been severally damaged.

Verse fourteen of the Third chapter of Genesis; the Lord deals with the sin and disobedience of man, and the death that had been pronounced on man. God would cause a resolution to the problem.

The Lord God said, unto the serpent, "Because thou hast done this, above all cattle, and above every beast of the field: upon the belly shalt thou go. And dust shall eat up all the days of thy life:

And I will put enmity between the woman. And between thy seed and her seed, it shall bruise thy head, and thy shalt bruise his heel."

Unto the woman he said, "I will greatly multiply thy sorrow and thy conception: in the sorrow thy shalt bring forth children: and thy desire shalt be to thy husband, and he shall rule over thee."

And unto Adam he said, "Because thou hast hearkened unto the voice of thy wife. And hast eaten of the tree which I commanded thee saying, thou shalt not eat of it, cursed is the ground for thy sake: in sorrow shalt thou eat of it all the days of thy life.

Thorns also and Thistles shall it bring forth to thee: and thou shalt eat the herbs of the fields:

In the sweat of thy face shalt thou eat bread, till thou return unto the ground: for out of it was thou taken: for didst thou eat, and unto dust shalt thou return".

(So the outcome of disobedience to God is death, by sin, a total reverse to none existence- death.)

The image of God's character is his likeliness and love, his holiness makes manifest his righteousness is powered by the Holy Spirit which brings love, joy, peace, longsuffering, gentleness, goodness, faith, meekness, and temperance.

All of these things were in Adam and Eve, it was their character.

Then come the serpent, who stole everything that God placed in man, even all creation on earth as God ruled on earth.

The image of God was changed for idols and it caused Adam and Eve to lose everything. The Lord God cast them out of the Garden of Eden to till the ground.

The Bible says:

"And he put a flaming sword with cherubim's (angels) to keep the way of the tree of life."

"Agallocha"

The Bible says: Genesis 3:22-24

"And the Lord God said, Behold, the man is become as one of us, to know good and evil, and now lest he put forth his hand, and take also of the tree of life, (AGALLOCHA) and live forever.

Therefore the Lord God sent him forth from the Garden of Eden, to till the ground from whence he was taken.

So he drove out the man: and he placed at the east of the Garden of Eden cherubim's, and a flaming sword which turned every way to keep the way of the tree of life." "Agallocha."

(These cherubims that God placed at the east of the Garden of Eden was there to keep Adam and Eve away from the tree of life. That tree had a fruit, with a seed, bearing a seed. This tree had been given a direct command from God to bear a fruit that produced life. Life that would never end. This tree assured that if you ate it, you would live forever. You could not die, nothing could kill you.

If Adam and Eve had eaten from this tree they would still be alive today in their present corrupt state.

Therefore corruption would have been uncontainable and unstoppable.

It was commanded by God, to this tree, to never die and all that would eat of it would live forever.

Chapter 8

"The trees of the Lord are full of sap; the cedars of Lebanon, which he hath planted.

As the valleys are they spread forth. As the gardens by, the rivers side, as the trees of lign aloes (Agallocha.) which he hath planted, and as cedar trees besides the waters." Jesus is the way, the truth, and the life.

God made a promise to man that he would bring forth a seed of the woman and it would bruise the devils head and that the seed of Satan would bruise Jesus' heel.

Jesus came to fulfill that promise and show us the way.

He came to restore all that the devil stole by public demonstration of the power of God. To restore our right to eat from the tree of life.

"The secret things belong unto the Lord our God: But those things which are revealed belong unto us and our children forever that we may do all the works of the law.

But God hath revealed them unto us by his Spirit : for the Spirit searcheth all things, yea. The deep things of God.

I saw now a dream which made me afraid, and the thoughts upon my bed and the visions of my head troubled me."

The Bible says: "Ask, and it shall be given you; seek, and ye shall find; Knock, and it shall be opened unto you. For every one that seeketh recieveth; And he that seeketh findeth: and to him that knocketh it shall be opened."
So I asked.

What if God will allow me to take a glimpse of the tree of life?
"Lord will you let me see this tree?"
Ask and it shall be given, seek and ye shall find.

When Adam and Eve received the sentence to death, it came in their children. Cain slew Able, and death began to reign.
The Bible says: and Adam knew Eve his wife and she conceived and bare Cain, and said I have gotten a man from the Lord.

And she again bear his brother Able. And Able was a keeper of sheep, but Cain was a tiller of the ground.

In process f time it came to pass, that Cain brought of the fruit of the ground an offering unto the Lord. And Able he also brought of the firstlings of his flock and of the fat thereof. And the Lord had respect unto Able and to his offering:
But unto Cain and his offering he had not respect. And Cain was very wroth and his countance fell.
And the Lord said unto Cain, "Why are thou wroth? and why is thy countenance fallen?

If thou doest well, shalt thou not be accepted? And if thou doest not well, sin lieth at the door. And unto thee shall be his desire, and it shalt rule over him."

Even to thee sin will lie and wait. God said even in cases where you are rebuked and your offering is rejected, when your countenance is fallen and revenge wants to take hold of you. You still have the ability to rebuke, turn away from, the schemes and tricks of the devil.

But even to this day, we don't seem to understand life. We can't seem to separate characters, the character of Satan from the character of Jesus.

How plain can it get. Jesus said, "I am come that you may have life, and that you might have it more abundantly. The thief cometh not, but for to steal and to kill and to destroy." What can be clearer?

The Bible says that: And Cain talked with Able his brother: and it came to pass, when they were in the field, that Cain rose up against Able his brother, and slew him. "Death began to reign." It was in control, and has had wide spread influence, on earth over man, as spoken by God in Genesis 3:19 as reads:

"In the sweat of thy face shalt thou eat bread, till thou return to the ground: for out of it wast thou taken: for dust thou art, and unto dust shalt thou return. He spake of Adam and Eve's death also.

But even before death came, God made a way back to himself, through the birth, death, and resurrection of Jesus his Son.

The serpent didn't know what death was. He couldn't have understood, even being cast out of heaven for rebelling against God".

Job 1:6b, tells us that Satan is able to go to and fro and stand before God in heaven.

Satan, or the serpent as he was called in Genesis three, did not know that death was a result of his none- reproduction.

He is only able to steal, kill, and destroy. Nothing that the devil does is able to do is to bring any thing lasting into existence. He can only destroy. He's a thief. He takes things that does not belong to him.

But remember, he's temporary.

He lied to Adam or I should say Eve. But Adam was right there when the conversation between the serpent and Eve took place.

He came to steal, but he can only fail.

He didn't know God as he thought he did when he said to Eve, ye shall not surely die: he didn't know what death was.

You must understand that the devil came from eternity with God, from his presence, unto time away from his presence, into a place fit for his final judgment to be cast him into hell.

There was no death in heaven. No sickness, even unto himself the devil didn't know that the power that he had worked toward his own destruction, so in setting Adam up, he made way for his own destruction, with his dominating power and influence.

The Bible says: "Only he that will let, will let."

How great are God's signs. How mighty are his wonders! His kingdom is an everlasting kingdom, and his dominion is from generation.

Chapter 9

I saw a dream which made me afraid. And thoughts upon my bed and visions of my head troubled me.

Thus were the visions of my head in my bed, I saw, and Behold, a tree in the midst of the earth, and the height thereof was great.

The tree grew, and was strong and the height thereof reached unto heaven, and the sight thereof to the end of all the earth:

The leaves thereof were fair, and the fruit thereof much, and it was meat for all the beast of the field had shadow under it, and the fowls of the heaven dwelt in the broughts thereof, and all flesh was fed of it.

Then there was a tree:
The waters made him great, the deep set of him up on high, with the rivers running about his plants, and set out her little rivers unto al the trees of the field.

Therefore his height was exalted above all the trees of the field, and his broughts multiplied, and his branches became long, because his multitude of waters, when he shot forth.

The fowls of heaven made their rests in his broughts, and under his branches did all the beasts of the field bring forth their young, and under his shadow dwelt all nations.

Thus was he fair in the greatness, in the length of his branches: for his root was by great waters.

The cedars in the garden of God could not hide him: the fig tree was not like his broughts, and the chestnut trees were not like his branches: nor any tree in the garden of God was like unto him in his beauty. (God said," I have made him fair by the multitude of his branches; so that all the trees of Eden, that were in the Garden of God, envied him.")

This tree was in the center of the garden of Eden. The tree of life was also in the midst of the garden of Eden.

Thus saith the LORD God, "Thou sealest up the sum, full of wisdom perfect in beauty.
This wisdom descended not from above, but earthy, sensual, devilish.

Thus has been in Eden the Garden of God; every precious stone was his covering, the sardis, topaz,, and the diamond, the beryl the onyx, and the jasper, the sapphire, the emerald, and the carbuncle, and gold: the workmanship of thy tabrets and of thy pipes thy pipes were prepared in thee in the day that thou were created.
Thou art the anointed cherub that covereth: I have set thee so: thou wast upon the holy mountain of God:
Thou hast walked up and down in the midst of the stones of fire;
Thou wast perfect in the day that thou was created, till iniquity was found in thee, By the multitude of thy merchandise they have filled

the midst of thee with violence, and thou hast sinned: therefore I will cast as profane out of the mountain of God: and I will destroy thee, O covering cherub, from the midst of the stones of fire.

Thine heart was lifted up because of thine beauty, thy hast corrupted thy wisdom by reason of thy brightness: I will lay thee to the ground, I will lay thee before kings, that they may behold thee.

(Jesus said, " I beheld satan as lightning fall from heaven".)

The Bible says that: And the great dragon was cast out, that old serpent, called the devil, and Satan, which deceiveth the whole world; he was cast out into the earth, and his angels were cast out with him.

And I heard a loud voice saying in heaven, "Now is come salvation; and strength, and power of his Christ: for the accuser of our brethren is cast down, which accuseth them before God day and night.

And they overcame him by the blood of the Lamb, and the word of their testimony; and they loved not their lives unto the death.

Therefore rejoice, ye heavens, and ye that dwell in them.

Woe to the inhibiters of the earth and of the sea; for the devil is come down unto you, having great wrath, because he knoweth that he hath but a short time."

The Bible says:

Thy pump is brought down to the grave, and the noise of thy viols: the worm is spread under thee.

How art thou fallen from heaven O Lucifer, son of the morning! How art thou cut down to the ground, which did weaken the nations!

For thou hast said in thy heart, I will ascend into heaven, I will exalt my throne above the stars of God: I will set upon the mount of the congregation, in the sides of the north:

I will ascend above the heights of the clouds: I will be like the Most High.

Yet thou shall be brought down to hell, to the sides of the pit.

They that see thee shall narrowly look upon thee, and consider thee, saying, Is this the man that made the earth to tremble, that did shake kingdoms:

That made the world as a wilderness, and destroyed the cities thereof; that opened not the house of the prisoners?

(By the multitude of the merchandise that satan has on earth has been filled with violence, what he has to offer from his self is total dishonor, shame, poverty, sickness and death. These things cause sin and when sin is finished it bringeth forth death.)

Chaptert 10

T he Bible says: Ask a sign of the LORD thy God; ask it either in-depth, or in the height above.
(So, I thought, "I wonder if this tree still exists today here on earth."

Then I asked the LORD God, "Does that tree exist today? Give us a glimpse of what it looks like. Not only that but what is the substance of it."

Jesus came that we might have life and that we might have it more abundantly and just as Adam did eat from the tree that was to regression, we must also eat from the tree of life.)

There is no jealousy coming from the tree of life. (AGALLOCHA)

The Bible says: Behold I will bring it health and cure, and I will cure them, and will reveal unto them the abundance of peace and truth.

And I will cause the captivity of Judah and the captivity of Israel to return, and I will build them, as at the first.

And I will cleanse them from all their iniquity whereby, whereby they have sinned against me: and I will pardon all their iniquities whereby they have transgressed against me.

And it shall be to me a name of joy, a praise and an honor before all nations of the earth, which shall hear all the good that I do unto them: And they shall fear and tremble for all the goodness and for all the prosperity that I procure unto it.

He hath said, which heard the words or God, which saw the vision of The Almighty, falling into a trance, but having his eyes open:

How goodly are thy tents, O Jacob, and thy Tabernacle, O Israel.

As valleys are spread forth, as gardens by the rivers side, as the trees of lign aloes which the Lord hath planted, as cedar trees besides the waters".

Agallocha – Botanical name_Aguiallaria

Agallocha – Agar wood –Lign Aloe tree.

The leaves are 5-9 cm. long, thinkly carcasses, oblong – lance state; the flowers are white, green, or dirty yellow in terminal sessile or shortly peduncled, umbellate cymes.

The scent that most are familiar with is obtained by water distillation from the oleoresin/wood, and have the scent of Lebanon.

This tree is found in varies southeast Asia forests, Bangladesh, Bengal, B'haton, Burma, China, Vietnam, and Cambodia and Africa.

The scent of this tree is remioscent of vetiver and the Bible says that it has a smell of Lebanon, it is said that it also smell like sandalwood and is extremely long lasting.

The Bible says. AND he shewed me a pure river of water of life, clean as crystal, proceeding out of the throne of God and of the Lamb.

In midst of the street of it, and on either side of the river, was there the tree of life. Which bear twelve manner of fruits, and yielded her fruit every month: and the leaves of the tree were for the healing of the nations. (**God is ready to finalize the process of the promise.**

Every aspect of this tree is for life, and for healing, it started with the tree of good and evil. And it ends with the tree of life.) And there shall be no more curse: but the throne of God and of the Lamb **(Jesus)** shall be in it: **and his servants shall serve him**: and they shall see his face: **and his name shall be in their forehead. Revelation 22:1 4**.

This tree, Agallocha, is used in traditional medical uses for: EVERYTHING the Bible says that it is for the healing of the nations. Not the Government, but for human consumption, asthma, chest congestion, colic, diarrhea, diuretic kidney problems, and nausea, thyroids, cancer, and lung tumors and as a general: Experience this oil by the hands of an anointed vessel of God, and receive your healing.

Agallocha! For the healing of the nations.

Jesus said,"I am come that they might have life, and that they might have it more abundantly. I am the good Shepard: the good Shepard giveth his life for the sheep,"

For God so loved the world, that he gave his only begotten Son, that whosoever believeth in him should not perish (die) but have everlasting (without interruption or end) life.

For God sent not his Son into the world to condemn the world: but that the world through him might be saved.

Jesus said: "For I have not spoken of myself; but the Father which sent me, he gave me commandment, what to say, and what I should speak.

And I know that his commandment is life everlasting: whatsoever I speak therefore, even as the Father said unto me, so I speak."

(And now the LORD is showing us, AGALLOCHA, He has commanded life unto us. He said; "Unto this people thou shalt say, Thus saith the LORD; Behold, I set before you the way of life, and the way of death.

Cast away from you all your transgressions; whereby ye have transgresses; and make you a new heart and a new spirit: for why would you die, O house of Israel?

For I have no pleasure in the death of him that dieth, saith the LORD GOD: Wherefore turn yourselves, and live ye," And the LORD GOD continued, "Say unto them, "I have no pleasure in the death of the wicked: but that the wicked turn from his way and live, turn ye, turn from your evil ways: for why will ye die, O house of Israel?"

In the visions of God, brought he me into the land of Israel, and sat me upon a very high mountain, by which was as the fame of a city on the south.

And he brought me thither, and, behold, there was a man, whose appearance was like the appearance of brass, with a line of flax in his hand, and a measuring reed; and he stood in the gate.

His head and his hairs was white like wool, as white as snow; and his eyes were as a flame of fire;
And his feet like unto fine brass, as if it had been burned in a furnace; and his voice as the sound of many waters.

And he said fear not: "I am the first and the last: I am he that liveth, and was dead; and, behold, I am alive forevermore. Amen, and have the keys of hell and death,"
O death, where is your sting? O grave, where is thy victory?
The sting of death is sin, and the sting of sin is the law. Behold the Lamb of God; which taketh away the sin of the world.

That as sin hath reigned unto death, even, so might grace reign through righteousness unto eternal life by Jesus Christ our Lord.
This is the bread which cometh down from heaven, that a man may eat thereof, and not die.
I am the living bread which came down from heaven: if any man eats of this bread, he shall live forever:

And the bread that I will give is my flesh, which I will give for the life of the world.

It is the spirit that quickeneth (that make alive) the flesh profeteth nothing; the words that I speak unto you they are Spirit, and they are life.

The thief cometh not, but for to steak, and to kill, and to destroy:

I am come that they might have life and have it more abundantly.

I am the good shepherd: the good shepherd giveth his life for the sheep."

Jesus said to Martha, "I am the resurrection and the life: he that believeth in me, though he were dead yet shall he live. And whosoever liveth and believeth in me shall never die.

Believest thou this?"

Jesus asked me if I believed that if we, or I believed in him, that I, or you would never die?

He had me to go to the dictionary and look up a few words that are so common and yet very powerful, we don't realize how powerful they are in the scripture.

Here they are: eternal, everlasting and never.

Now I invite you to read this revelation knowledge for yourselves.

Jesus said, "Whosoever liveth, (that means, who ever is alive to day) and believeth in me. (To believe is to agree with, stand by, take up residence and abide, become unshakable, un-removable). Shall never die."

Never die: this word never- means: in no way, not at all, on no occasion. shall never is with a commanded promise.

Jesus said, "This commandment is life everlasting." Everlasting means; lasting forever, continuing on in life: this eternal command is from God and cannot go unfulfilled.

Jehovah himself, has commanded us to have authority to exercise the ability to have a dwelling place for the **HOLY SPIRIT** to dwell, which is our bodies.)

To receive the Holy Spirit is to receive life back from the dead, this command is direct with authority. The HOLY SPIRIT comes bearing gifts, to empower us for the work of the kingdom of God.

When Jesus died on the cross at Calvary, redemption was so powerful that it could not go unfulfilled by the saints of God that had already fallen asleep (died).

They lived again, broke open their graves and lived!

The Bible says: Now that he ascended, what is it but that he also descended first into the lower parts of the earth?

He that descended is the same that also ascended far above all heavens, that he might fulfill all things.

When Jesus said, "It is finished", he fulfilled the promise of our redemption to restoration to life, and not to death but for us to live, just as Cain fulfilled the promise to the curse to death. Jesus has redeemed us from the curse of death. We must receive the benefits of the promises, that is fulfilled by Jesus; of restoration to life.)

The Bible says that:

Jesus when he had cried again with a loud voice. Yield up the ghost. (He gave the Holy Spirit permission to depart).

And behold, the veil of the temple was rent in twain from the top to the bottom; and the earth did quake, and the rocks rent;

And the graves were opened: and many bodies of the saints which slept arose;

And came out of the graves, after his resurrection, and went into the holy city, and appeared to many. (This prophesy fulfilled the scripture prophesy in Hosea 13:14.

"I will ransom them from the power of the grave: I will redeem them from death:

O death I will be thy plagues: O grave I will be thy destruction."

(When I thought to know this it was too painful for me. Until I went into the sanctuary of God: then understood I their end.)

Chapter 11

T he Bible says; THERE was a man of the Pharisees, named Nicodemus, a ruler of the Jews:

He same came to Jesus by night, and said unto him, Rabbi, we know that thou art a teacher come from God: for no man can do these miracles that thou doest, except God be with him.

Jesus answered and said unto him. "Verily, verily I say unto thee, except a man be born again, he cannot see the kingdom of God."

Nicodemus saith unto him, "How can a man be born when he is old? Can he enter the second time into his mother's womb, and be born?"

Jesus answered, "Except a man be born of water and of Spirit, he cannot enter into the kingdom of God."

(Entering the kingdom of God? Let's see just exactly what is the kingdom of God.

In order to enter into the kingdom of God we must be able to see it, no, not physically, but see the vision of the of the kingdom of God spiritually; to be able to enter into it. We have to want to live the way

God has ordained for us to live, and desire to operate under God's leadership.

We must be able to see and accept, God kingdom coming right here on earth. If we can't accept his guidance now right here, how on earth do we think that we will make heaven our home.

We first must accept the fact that restoration to life is available to us now. We have the power to accept life right here on earth, we must reject the weapon that the devil defeats us with, and that is death.

We must receive the power that was restored to us, by God's Spirit. That same Spirit that raised up Christ from the dead, that Spirit dwells in you, and if that Spirit dwells in you that Spirit cannot die.

We must accept the dominion that God has made us overseers of: and that is earth.

Nation after nation is fighting over territory on earth and cannot live in harmony with each other here, so what do they want to do, go to heaven and change heaven also, we can't even live in peace on earth.

But we can live in peace, when we follow Christ we will have peace.

Your image must be restored, Jesus died to transfer the title deed, and all rights to your claim, to reestablish us as sons of God. It's God's plan to restore all that the devil stole, He has made available to us, the ability to love again, have power, he has restored our minds; when we allow our minds to be fully restored by his Spirit we will trust him.

We need to go behind the torn veil, it is there we will find very clear directions, it is a hereditary privilege by the Spirit.)

"For the law of the Spirit of life in Christ Jesus has made me free from the law of sin and death.

For what the law could not do, in that it was weak through the flesh, God sending his own Son in the likeness of sinful flesh, and for sin: condemning sin in the flesh.

That the righteousness of the law might be fulfilled in us, who walk not after the flesh, but after the Spirit.

For they that are after the flesh: do mind the things of the flesh; but they after the Spirit the things of the Spirit.

For to be carnally minded is death; Because the carnal mind is enmity against God: for it is not subject to the law of God, neither indeed can be.

So then they that are in the flesh cannot please God;

But ye are not in the flesh, but in the Spirit, if so be that the Spirit of God dwell in you. Now if any man have not the Spirit of God he is none of his.

And if Christ be in you, the body is dead because of sin:

(In the path of righteousness is life: and in the pathway thereof, there is no death.) That's why the Bible says, But if the Spirit of him that raised up Christ from the dead dwell in you, he that rose up Christ from the dead shall also quicken (make alive) your mortal bodies by the Spirit that dwelleth in you. (The Spirit gives you strength to continue to live free from the strength of any deadly or other wise disease.)

Therefore, brethren, we are debtors not to the flesh, to live after the flesh". (I am not in debt to the flesh to present my body, soul, or Spirit before witnesses to sin, that any claims can be demanded for my soul, holding my life as collateral by the creditor, which is the devil.

He will show you a world of a time. If you do what he beguiles you to do: In exchange for your soul.

So if you play with him, just remember he will want to play back.

He only wants to draw you out, way out! away from God.

Jesus has guaranteed the pledge, and said the price of the demand that held death, hell, and the grave.

Jesus is the ransom that was paid. It is paid in full, and Jesus has the keys to death hell and the grave.

Now you have the gift of life presented to you. That you might take of the 'Tree of Life (**AGALLOCHA**) and eat freely."

So the free gift is to life. To continue in life, is what Jesus came to make a way to.

Jesus came and showed us the way. He showed us love and compassion, how we should be willing to let love flow freely from us. He showed us how to perform with power and how to enter into eternity.

"Because just as death reigned, so also shall life reign."

That as sin hath reigned unto death, even so might grace reign through righteousness unto eternal life by Jesus Christ our Lord." Romans 5:21.

God has commanded us to live, and the devil is still lying and telling you that you must die to get to God. Death is not God's friend to get you to him, awake out of darkness, and come and sit under the light, that you might see.

There is nothing that Satan can present to you, that you should be willing to die for. He works under the covering of sin; and when sin is finished, it brings forth death. No sin, no death, Jesus made a way to escape sin.

The Bible says,

"What saith it? The word is nigh thee, even in thy mouth, and in thy heart: that is the word of faith, which we preach;

That if thou shalt confess with thy mouth the Lord Jesus, and believe in thine heart that God hath raised him from the dead, thou shalt be saved.

For with the heart man believeth unto righteousness: and confession is made unto salvation."

Jesus died for the sins of the world. He is the cure for every disease. He came to demonstrate life, and give us ways to remain alive until he comes and destroys last enemy of God, which is death.

We have the God given authority and power to rebuke death and all kinds of sickness.

The Bible says, "But we have this power in earthen vessels, that the excellency of the power might be of God and not us."
All things Jesus did was to show us life.
Through faith and the words written in the Bible.

That by faith you might hear and be saved and live.
He has showed us how to speak a word of love and compassion, lay hands on the sick, and their health be restored.
All of this is done by the Spirit of God working in us; being filled with the fullness of God will manifest his power, working in us.

He has given us joy for laughter, it is strong medicine, love and compassion for faith, hope for the assurance of a cure, and salvation.

"As Moses lifted up the serpent in the wilderness, even so must the Son of man be lifted up.
That whosoever believeth in him should not perish (die) but have everlasting life." (without interruption or end)

The Bible says that: Because of the way, the children of Israel had to travel; they became discouraged because of the way.
The Bible says:
And they journeyed from mount Hor by way of The Red Sea, to compass the land of Edom: and the soul of the people was much discouraged because of the way.

And the people spake against God, and against Moses, "Wherefore have ye brought us up out of Egypt to die in the wilderness? For there is no bread, neither is there any water: and our soul loatheth this light bread."

And the Lord sent fiery serpents among the people, and much of the people of the children of Israel died.

Therefore the people came to Moses, and said, "We have sinned, for we have spoken against the Lord, and against thee; pray unto the Lord, that he take away the serpents from us." And Moses prayed for the people.

And the Lord said unto Moses, "Make thee a fiery serpent, and set it upon a pole: and it shall come to pass, that every one that is bitten, when he looketh upon it shall live."
And the Bible says that, Moses made a serpent of brass, and put it upon a pole, and it came to pass. That if a serpent had bitten any man, when he beheld the serpent of brass, he lived.

God didn't take the serpents away, they repented unto life, and a way of sustaining life was made. They looked at what caused their death, and lived. God made a way of life.
God always establishes his word. What ever he says: is.

Now God has, through his ministers, no matter who they are, male or female, as long as they have been chosen by God; (**AND BELIEVE THAT HE IS GOD**) he has established healing.

The Bible says. Numbers 16:4-50.
But on the marrow all the congregation of the children of Israel murmured against Moses, and against Aaron saying,
"Ye have killed the people of the Lord, and it came to pass, when the congregation was gathered against Moses and against Aaron, that they looked toward the tabernacle of the congregation: and, behold, the cloud covered it, and the glory of the Lord appeared,

And Moses and Aaron came before the tabernacle of the congregation,

And the Lord spake unto Moses, saying, "Get ye up from among this congregation, that I may consume them as in a moment." And they fell upon their faces. And Moses said unto Aaron, "Take a censer and put fire therein from off the altar, and put on incense and go quickly upon the congregation, and make an Atonement for them, for there is wrath gone out from the Lord; the plague is begun."

And Aaron took as Moses commanded and ran into the midst of the congregation; and, behold, the plague was begun among the people; and he put on incense and made an atonement for the people.

And he stood between the dead and the living; and the plague was stayed. (Aaron separated death from life; he caused death to cease from among the people.)

The Bible says that, Now they that died in the plague were fourteen thousand and seven hundred, besides them that died about the matter of Korah.

And Aaron returned unto Moses, unto the door of the tabernacle of the congregation: and the plague was stayed.

And the Lord, spake unto Moses saying, "Speak unto the children of Israel and take of everyone of them a rod, according to the house of their fathers of al their princes, according to the house of their fathers, of all the princes according to the house of their fathers twelve rods: write thou every man's name upon his rod.

And thou shalt write Aaron's name upon the rod of Levi: for a rod shall be for the head of the house of their fathers.

And thou shall lay them up in the tabernacle of the congregation before the testimony, where I will meet with you.

And it shall come to pass, that the man's rod, whom I should choose, shall bloom; and I will make cease from me the murmuring of the children of Israel, whereby they murmur against you."

And Moses spake unto the children of Israel and every one of their princes gave him a rod, a piece, for each prince one, according to their father's houses, even twelve rods: and the rod of Aaron was among their rods.

And Moses laid up the rod before the Lord in the tabernacle of witness.

And it came to pass, on the marrow Moses went into the tabernacle of witness; and behold, the rod of Aaron for the house of Levi was budded (it had came to life) and brought forth buds (showed production) and bloomed (the beauty was restored) blossoms and yielded Almonds. (it went into full productivity, dead broken off coming back to life to show full restoration.)

And Moses brought out all the rods from before the Lord unto the children of Israel: and they looked, and took every man his rod. And the Lord said unto Moses, "Bring Aaron's rod again before the testimony, to be kept for a token against the rebels; and thou shall quite take away their murmuring from me, that they die not.

For this commandment which I command thee this day, it is not hidden from thee, neither is it far off.

It is not in heaven, that thou shouldest say, who shall go up for us to heaven and bring it unto us that we may hear it and do it?

Neither is it beyond the sea, that thou shouldest say, who should go over the sea for us, and bring it unto us, that we may hear it and do it? But the word is very nigh unto thee, in thy mouth, and in thy heart, that thou mayest do it.

See, I have set before thee this day life and good, and death and evil.

In that I command thee this day to, love the LORD thy God, to walk in his ways, and keep his commandments, and his statues, and his judgments, that thou mayest live and multiply, and the Lord thy God shall bless thee in the land whether thou goest to possess it.

I call heaven and earth to record this day against you, that I have set before you life and death, blessing and cursing: therefore choose life, that both you and your seed shall live." (It is absolutely clear God commands life, and not death.)

Chapter 12

Elijah raised the dead to keep the vision of God visible.

The Bible says, one Kings 17:21-24.

And he cried unto the Lord, and said, "O LORD my God, has thou brought evil upon the woman with whom I sojourn, by slaying her son?"

And he stretched himself upon the child three times, and cried unto the LORD, and said, O LORD my God, I pray thee, let this child's soul come to him again, and he revived (lived).

And Elijah took the child and brought him down out of the chamber into the house, and delivered him unto his mother, and Elijah said, "See, thy son liveth."

And the woman said unto Elijah, "Now by this I know that thou art a man of God, and that the word of the LORD, in thy mouth is truth."

(When I thought to know this about AGALLOCHA and life ever-lasting, living forever, not dying, because of our unbelief in what God has already done and what he is waiting to do; it was joy to my heart.

Chapter 13

The Bible says that, but it is written, " Eye hath not seen, nor ear heard, neither have entered into the hart of man, the things which God hath prepared for him that love him. But God has revealed them by his Spirit: for the Spirit searches all things yea the deep things of God".

AGALLOCHA, lign aloes, the tree that flourishes by the river of water. Ezekiel 47:7-9, 12.

And when I had returned; behold. At the brink of the river there were very many trees on the one side and on the other.

Then said he unto me, "These waters issue out towards the east country, and go down into the desert, and go into the sea: which be-ing brought forth into the sea, the waters shall be healed.

And it shall come to pass, that everything that liveth, which moveth, whethersoever the rivers shall come, shall live: and there shall be a very great multitude of fish, because these waters shall come thither: for they shall be healed: and everything shall live whether the river cometh.

And by the river upon the bank thereof, on this side and on that side shall grow all trees for meat (AGALLOCHA) whose leaves shall not fade, neither shall the fruit thereof be consumed: it shall bring forth new fruit according to his months, because their waters they issue out of the sanctuary and the fruit thereof shall be for meat, and the leave thereof for medicine." The fruit and the leaves of Agallocha will heal every disease that can be named and unnamed

AGALLOCHA: (Lign Aloe). AGALLOCHA releases an aroma that unfolds over a period of twelve hours, there is no other known oil that is this tenacious, as a smell of Labanon.

O ISRAEL, return unto the Lord thy God; for thou has fallen by thine own iniquity. Take with you words and turn to the Lord: say unto him, Take away all iniquity, and receive us graciously, so will we render the calves of our lips.

Asher shall not save us; we will not ride upon horses: neither will we say any more to the work of our hands, ye are our gods: for in thee the fatherless find mercy.

Thus saith the LORD,"I will heal thy backsliding, I will love them freely for my anger is turned away from him.

I will be as the dew unto Israel: he shall grow as the lily, and cast forth his roots as Lebanon."

" When I thought to know this, it was too painful for me."

And again, I heard this word" Agallocha", then the Lord said, "Write the vision and make it plain up on tables, that he may run that readeth it." He said,

"I will ransom them from the power of the grave: I will redeem them from death, I will be thy plagues: O grave, I will be thy destruction: repentance is hid from mine eyes." (The tree with the smell of Lebanon, Agallocha: a tiny bit of this oil sends an aroma that lasts for twelve hours, no other oil with the beauty of life and this smell, lasts as long.)

The Bible says:

They that dwell under his shadow shall return: they shall revive as the corn, and grow as the vine: the scent thereof shall be as the wine of Lebanon.

Ephraim shall say, "What have I to do any more with idols? I have heard him, and observed him: I am like a green fir tree. From me is thy fruit found."

The Bible says, "For he shall be as a tree planted by the waters, and that spreadeth out her roots by the river, and shall not see when heat cometh, but her leaf shall be green: and shall not be careful in the year of drought, neither shall cease from yielding fruit.

It shall bring forth new fruit according to his months, because their waters they issue out of the sanctuary: and the fruit thereof shall be for meat, and the leaf thereof for medicine.

As the valleys are they spread forth as gardens of the river side, as the trees of lign aloes which the Lord hath planted. And as the cedar trees beside the waters."

I say to you, "God has left nothing undone. We must walk in life just as Cain and Able walked out the curse of death.

Jesus has paid the price, It is finished! Now we must walk out the blessings to life eternal".

I say to you that, "God has blessed you with this promise."

AND he showed me a pure river of water of life, clear as crystal, proceeding out of the throne of God and out of the LAMB.

In the midst of the street of it, and on either side of the river, was Agallocha (the tree of life) which bear twelve manner of fruits, and yield her fruit every month: and the leaves of the tree were for the healing of the nations.)

Blessed are they that do his commandments, that they may have right to (Agallocha) the tree of life, and may enter in through the gates into the city.

Chapter 14

Now faith is the substance of things hoped for, the evidence of things not seen for by it the elders obtain a good report. Thought faith we understand that the worlds were formed by the word of God, so that things which are seen were not made of things which do appear.

The Bible says:

But ye are come unto mount Sion and unto the city of the living God, the heavenly Jerusalem, and to an unnumerable company of angels.

To the general assembly of church of the first born, which is written in heaven, and to God the judge of all, and to the spirits of just men made perfect.

And to Jesus the mediator of the new covenant, and to the blood a sprinkling, that speaketh better things than that of Able.

See that you refuse not him that speaketh. For if they escaped not who refused him that spake on earth, much more shall not we escape if we turn away from him that speaketh from heaven:

Whose voice then shook thee earth: but now he hath promised, saying, Yet once more I shake not the earth only, but also heaven.

And this word, Yet once more signifieth the removing of those things that are shaken, as of things that are made, that those things which cannot be shaken may remain".

By faith Able offered unto God a more excellent sacrifice than Cain, by which he attained witness that he was righteous.

God testifying of his gifts: and by it he being dead yet speaketh.

By faith Enoch was translated that should not see death; and was not found because God translated him (went to heaven alive) for before his translation he had this testimony that he pleased God. but without faith it is impossible to please him: for he that cometh to God must believe that he is, and that he is a rewarder of them that diligently seek him.

By faith, Noah being warned of God, by things not been yet, move with fear, prepared an arc of his house, by which he condemned the world, and became the air of the righteousness which is by faith.

By faith Abraham, when he was called to go out into a place which he should after receive for an inheritance, obeyed: and he went out: not knowing whether he went,

By faith he sojourned in the land of promise, as in a strange country, dwelling in tabernacles with Isaac and Jacob, the heirs with him of the same promise:

For he looked for a city which hath foundations, whose builder and maker is God.

Through faith also Sarah herself receive strength to conceive seed, and was delivered of a child when she was past age, because she judged him faithful who had promised.

Therefore sprang there even of one, and him as good as dead, so many as the stars of the sky in multitude, and as the sand is by the sea shore innumerable.

These all died in faith not having received the promise but having seen them afar off, and were persuaded of them, and embrace them, and confessed that they were strangers and pilgrims on the earth.

For they that say such things declare plainly that they seek a country.

And truly, if they had been mindful of that country from whince they came out, they might have had opportunity to have returned.

But now they desire a better country that is, an heavenly: wherefor God is not ashamed to be called their God: for he hath prepared for them a city.

By faith Abraham, when he was tried, offered up Isaac: and he that had received the promise offered up his only begotten Son.

Of whom it was said, that in Isaac shall thy seed be called:

Accounting that God was able to raise him up, even from the dead; from whince also he received him in a figure.

By faith Isaac blessed Jacob and Esau concerning things to come.

By faith Jacob, when he was a dying blessed both the sons of Joseph; and worshipped, leaning upon the top of his staff.

By faith Moses when he was born, was hid three months by his parents because they saw he was a proper child: and they were not afraid of the king's commandment.

By faith Moses when he was come to years, refused to be called the son of Pharaoh's daughter.

Choosing rather to suffer affliction with the people of God, than to enjoy pleasure of sin for a season,

Esteeming the reproach of Christ greater riches than the treasures of Egypt: for he had respect unto thee recompence of the reward.

By faith he forsook Egypt, not fearing the wrath of the king: for he endured, as seeing him who is invisible.   Through faith he keeps the Passover, and the sprinkling of blood, lest he that destroyed the firstborn should touch them.

By faith they passed through the red sea as by dry land: which the Egyptians assaying to do were drowned.

By faith Joseph, when he died, made mention of the departing of the children of Israel: and gave commandment concerning his bones. (he knew that God is faithful, he did not want his bones left in Egypt under bondage he wanted them carried into the promise land.)

The Bible says: Exodus13:19.

And Moses took the bones of Joseph with him: for he had straightly sworn the children of Israel, saying, "God will surely visit you and ye shall carry up my bones away hence with you." (so it is clear that Joseph saw the promise.)

By faith the walls of Jericho fell down, after they were compassed about seven days.

By faith the harlot Rehab perished not with them that believeth not, when she had received the spies with peace,

And what should I more say? For the time would fail me to tell of Gideon, and Barack and Samson, and Jephthae; of David also, and Samuel, and of the prophets:

Who through faith subdued kingdoms, wrought righteousness, obtained promises, stopped the mouths of lions, quenched the violent fire, escaped the edge of the sword, out of weakness were made strong, waxed valiant in fight, turned to fight the armies of the aliens.

Women received their dead to life again: others were tortured. Not accepting deliverance; that they might obtain a better resurrection.

And others had trial of cruel mockings and scourging, Yea, moreover of bonds and imprisonment:

They were stoned sown asunder, tempted, were slain with the sword: they wondered about in sheep skins and goat skins, being destitute, affected, tormented;

Of whom the world was not worthy: they wondered in deserts, in mountains, and in dens and in caves of the earth.

And these having obtained a good report through faith. (which is the strength of hope, because hope maketh not ashamed.) receive not the promise;

God having provided some better thing for us, that they without us shall not be made perfect. (they were willing to suffer, and wait, and not leave us out the promises of God. Alleluia! Alleluia! Thank you God!)

WHEREFORE seeing we also are compassed about with so great a cloud (sure covering) of witnesses, let us lay aside every weight and the sin which does so easily beset us, and let us run with patience the race that is set before us,

Looking unto Jesus thee author and finisher of our faith: who for the joy that was set before him endure the cross, despising the shame, and set down at the right hand of God,

Seeing then that we have a great high Priest, that is passed into the heavens,

Jesus the Son of God let us hold fast our profession.

For we have not a high Priest which cannot be touched with the feelings of our infirmities; but was in all points tempted as like we are, Yet without sin.

Chapter 15

The Bible says in Matthew 26:36-46.

Then cometh Jesus with them into a place called Gethsemene, and he say unto his disciples, "Sit ye hear, while I go and pray yonder." And he took with him Peter and the two sons of Zebedee, and began to be sorrowful and very heavy then say he unto them, "My soul is exceeding sorrowful even unto death: tarry ye here and watch with me."

And he went a little further, and fell on his face, and prayed, saying, "O my Father, if it be possible, let this cup pass from me: Nevertheless not as I will, but as thou wilt."

And he cometh unto the disciples, and findeth him them asleep, and saith unto Peter, "What, could ye not watch with me one hour?

Watch and pray, that ye enter not into temptation the spirit indeed is willing, but the flesh is weak."

He went away again the second time and prayed, saying, "O my Father, if this cup may not pass away from me, except I drink it, thy will be done."

And he came and found them asleep again for their eyes were heavy.

And he left them, and went away again, and prayed the third time, saying the same words.

Then cometh he unto his disciples, and saith unto them. "Sleep on now, and take your rest; behold, the hour is at hand and the Son of man is betrayed into the hands of sinners. Rise, let us be going: behold, he is at hand that doest betray me."

What is in this cup?

Thus saith the Lord, The Holy One of Israel and his Maker; "Ask me of things to come concerning my sons, and the works of my hands command ye me."

So I asked; "What is in that cup of the called?"

Suddenly as I looked, I saw, behold; every form of creeping thing, and abominable beast.

And I look closer, and I saw the creeping things and the abominable beast were mingled together, struggling in their own filthy excrement.

Each vile creeping thing represented an avenue of sin, the maggots and what seemed like earth worms mingled their deterating bodies: the beast and creeping things of some I could not rightly receive, all mingling and embracing themselves in fornication, adultery, witchcraft, murders, sorcery, idolaters, and men lovers of themselves, and women lovers of themselves, these were some of us.

As I look the creeping crawling things didn't seem to know that they could be delivered so they continued in sin.

Behold, I looked and the creeping things had covered there a body, they had clothed themselves there; as they made a habitation of sin, they moved about among the clots of dirt or dust a dark, murky, stinking, slimy, substance with a bloody stream in it.

Then I looked again, and I saw there a face, a pitiful sight. It lay in agony and pain, as the creeping crawling things; feasted themselves on the flesh of torn flesh, mingled sores with pulse running from them.

I looked even closer and each one had faces, there was an unnumerable amount of bodies, then! I looked and there was one that I recognized, it was my face.

Then I saw the brightness of one like the Son of God, covered the cup, there was a great relief then when he was present then when he withdrew himself: agony returned.

When Jesus looked into the cup the creeping crawling things stopped devouring the flesh. It was then that the spirit and soul was relieved.

Jesus moved away again, and the creeping crawling things and evil beasts, continue their taunting, and devouring the flesh,

Then one like the Son of God, came again and covered the cup again. Then there was relief again, because the creeping crawling beast could not devourer when the Son of God's face was present.

Then I realized that each time the presence of the Lord was there, there was relief.

I began to look up, look up, look up waiting with great anticipation to see the face of Jesus again: I realized that the creeping crawling things the beasts, even in all their devouring had no powers over me or anyone when Jesus was present.

There was no time to wonder about why he kept moving away. All I knew was I wanted him to come back, when he was absent the torment and agony started again.

In my agony, I cried, "Lord to what purpose have you created me, what good am I, why have I come into this world? Forgive me for all my sins"

Then the face of Jesus appeared the third time. This time it was different than the times before.

He had been refreshed and strengthened, the stench of sin, hell and the grave didn't seem to bother him this time.

He picked up the cup, and he drank the sins of the world, that he might take sin to the cross.

As I entered his presence he consumed me, relief came immediately, a renewing of my body took place, I was strengthened, he restored my soul, I was cleansed and made whole, to love, more, have compassion to love thy brethren, having the ability to forgive, and not hold unforgiveness against anyone.

The creeping crawling things were now contained by the power in Jesus.

God's will had taken place; Jesus could not just drink the cup of sin, he is holy and righteous, he knows no sin. He had to earnestly pray that the Father's will be done. He had to lay aside his will to drink: that God's will be done.

He said, "Not my will: but thy will be done."
When Jesus said unto his disciples, "My soul is exceeding sorrowful, even unto death, tarry ye hear, and watch with me."
What Jesus is experiencing is, both men and the divine deity, of God.

The Bible says,
And the word was made flesh, and dwelt among us, and we beheld his glory as the only begotten of the Father, full of grace and truth.
So what I saw when Jesus overshadowed the cup was a sorrow felt for the sinful world, as he, struggled to lay aside his own holiness to drink sin.

He knew that sorrow would remain with him even to death. his death for me and you, that we may have life.

Let (permit) life reign, it must reign. God commanded life to reign (to be in control). If you say life cannot take control of death, you say that Jesus nor his death is of none effect.

Chapter 16

"For there is hope of a tree, if it be cut down, that it will sprout again, and the tender branch thereof will not cease.

Though the root thereof wax old in the earth, and the stock thereof die in the ground. Yet through the scent of water it will bud, and bring froth broughts like a plant,

As the valleys are spread forth, as gardens by the rivers side, as the trees of Lign Aloes, (Agallocha) which the Lord hath planted and as cedar trees beside the waters. (He shall pour the water out of his bucket and his seed shall be in many waters, uncontainable!)

Thus were the visions of mine head in mine bed; I saw, and behold a in the midst of the earth, and the height thereof was great. Whose leaf shall not fade, neither shall the fruit thereof be consumed (never run out): it shall bring forth new fruit according to his months, because their waters they issue out of the sanctuary: and the fruit thereof shall be for meat and the leaf thereof for medicine.

"He that has an ear, let him hear, what the Spirit saith unto the churches: to him that overcometh will I give to eat the hidden manna, and will give him a white stone, and in the stone a new name written, which no man knoweth saving he that recieveth it.

He that hath an ear let him hear what the Spirit saith unto the churches: to him that overcometh will I give to eat of the Tree of Life (Agallocha), which

Is in the midst of the paradise of God."

The Bible says.

"For since by man came death, by man also the resurrection of the dead.

For in Adam all die, even so in Christ shall all be made alive."

If ye have heard of the dispensation of the grace of God, which is given to you ward:

How by revelation he made known unto me the mystery; (as I wrote a afore in few words,

Whereby, when you read, you may understand my knowledge in the mystery of Christ. For I determined not to know any thing among you, save Jesus Christ and him crucified.

And I was with you in weakness, and in fear, and inn much trembling.

And my speech and my preaching was not with enticing words of man's wisdom, but in demonstration of the Spirit and of power. That your faith should not stand in the wisdom of men, but in the power of God.)

Which in other ages is were not made known unto the sons of man, as it is now revealed unto his holy apostles and prophets by the Spirit.

That the Gentiles should be fellowheirs, and of the same body and partaker of hi promise in Christ by the gospel; whereby I was made a minister according to the gift of the grace of God given unto me by the effectual working of his power.

Unto me, who is less than the least of all saints, is this grace given, that I should preach among the Gentiles the unsearchable riches of Christ:

And make all men see what is the fellowship of the mystery, which from the beginning of the world had been hid in God, who created all things by Jesus Christ.

To the intent that now unto the principalities and powers in heavenly places might be known by the church the manifold wisdom of God, according to thee eternal purpose which he purposed in Christ Jesus our Lord;

In whom we have boldness and access with confidence by faith with him,

For the fruit of the Spirit is all goodness and righteousness and truth:

But now is made manifest by the appearing of our Saviour Jesus Christ, who has abolished death, (counteracted the force and the effectiveness of it.) and has brought life and immortality to light through the gospel.

For if by one man's offence death reign by one; Much more they which receive abundance of grace and the gift of righteousness shall reign in life by one, the free gift came upon all men unto justification of life.

For by one man's disobedience many were made sinners so by the obedience of one shall many be made righteous

In the way of righteousness; and in the pathway thereof there is no death.

Moreover the law entered, that the offence might abound.

But where sin abounded, grace did much more abound.

That as in reigned unto death, even so might grace reign through righteousness unto eternal life by Jesus Christ our Lord.

For if you life after the flesh, ye shall die: but if you through the Spirit do mortify the deeds of the body, ye shall live.

Jesus said, "The thief cometh not but for to steal, to kill, and to destroy: I am come that they might have life, and that they might have it more abundantly."

For God so loved the world that he gave his only Begotten Son, that whosoever believeth in him shall no it perish, but have everlasting life.

-"LIVE YE LIVE"-

Death came into the world by Cain and Able because of the sin of Adam and Eve.

Life is restored for us in Jesus Christ.

God made a way for us to be restored, and walk and live in his image.

The Bible says that;

The cherubim's had been placed east of the Garden of Eden to keep the way of the tree of life.

Jesus died and God raised him from the dead that is what gives us the right to eat of the hidden manna and eat of the tree of life. (Agallocha)

When I asked, God gave me Agallocha! There is none other tree like unto this tree, everything about his tree has healing properties, so I say to you, "Please gain the victory: overcome death, with righteousness, again I say to you, and I cannot stress the points enough for you to get it, that: In the way of righteousness is life, and in the pathway thereof there is no death."

Chapter 17

By faith Peter and John was moved with compassion. And the man that lie at the gate beautiful was healed.

By faith they sent for Peter, when Darcus died, by faith Peter did what he saw Jesus do. And Darcus lived.

By faith many were laid in the streets and the shadow of Peter healed everyone, no matter what their diseases were.

By faith Paul was preaching long, and Eutechrist fell out the window and died, By faith, Paul went down and raised him to life.

Now by faith, Agallocha: will heal every sickness and disease when used by God's appointed ministers to prepare man for eternity.

(Because we are under a dispensation from God it is an allotted time in which we are entered, a time where we are answerable to God: for how we have heard and obeyed the revelation of the gospel (the good news) after hearing it.

Do we accept the truth and allow Jesus to reign or do we still want Satan to be in control of earth?)

You must bear the mark of the only true God in your forehead (the Holy Ghost's in dwelling)
So shall life begin to reign when righteousness and peace kiss each other.

And he shall judge among the nations and shall rebuke many people: and they shall beat their swords into plowsherers into pruning hooks: nations shall not lift up sword against nation: neither shall they learn war anymore.

The Bible says.
And they shall go into the holes of the rocks, and into the caves of the earth for fear of the Lord, and for the glory of his majesty, when he arises to shake terribly the earth.

In that day a man shall cast his idols of silver, and his idols of gold, which they had made each one for himself to worship; to the moles and to the bats:
To go into the cliff of the rocks, and unto the tops of the ragged rocks, for fear of the Lord and for that glory of his majesty when he arises to shake terribly the earth.
And the kings of the earth, and the great men, and the rich men, and the chief captains, and the mighty men, and every bondman, and every freeman, hid themselves in the dens and in the rocks of the mountains:
And said to the mountains and rocks, "Fall on us, and hid us from the face of him that setteth on the throne and from the wrath of the Lamb.
For the great day of his wrath is come: and who shall be able to stand?"

And in those days shall men seek death, and shall not find it; and desire to die, and death shall flee from them.

At this point, time has ended and eternity has began.

Righteousness and peace coming together, two people that will meet together to bring in eternity.

Then you will hear of accidents that should have been fatal, and everyone lived.

But woe! to them that has not received salvation through our Lord and Saviour Jesus Christ; they will remain in that state forever separated from God or the opportunity to be saved.

For there will be time no longer, eternity has begun, there will be no party in hell.

The Bible says.

And the angel which I saw stand upon the sea and upon the earth and lifted up his hand to heaven.

And swear by him that liveth forever and ever, who created heaven and the things that there in are, and the earth, and the things which are there in, that, "there shall be time no longer."

But in the days of the voice of the seventh angel, when he shall begin to sound, the mystery of God should be finished, as he has declared to his servants the prophets.

And the rest of the men which were not killed by these plagues yet repented not of the works of their hands, that they should not worship devils and idols of gold and silver and of brass, and stone, and of wood: which neither can see nor hear, nor walk:

Neither repented they of their murders, nor of heir sorceries, nor of their fornication, nor of their thief's,

And they had a king over them, which is the angel of the bottomless pit whose name in the Hebrew tongue is Abadon, but in the Greek tongue hath his name Apollyon.

One woe is passed; and, behold, there come two woes more thereafter.

The Bible says; to have the right to the tree of; life you must repent of your sins and turn from darkness to light.

The Bible says; But what saith it? "The word is nigh thee, even in thy mouth and in thy heart, that is the word, of which we preach:

That if thou shalt confess with thy mouth the Lord Jesus and shall believe in thy heart that God hath raised him from the dead, thou shalt be saved. For with the heart man believeth unto righteousness and with the mouth confession is made unto salvation."

Chapter 18

Hold fast the form of sound words, which thou hast heard of me, in faith and love which is in Christ Jesus.
Do not miss salvation.
He that overcometh shall have a right to eat of the tree of life.

HELL is real. The fire is never quenched.
There was a certain rich man which was clothed in purple and fine linen, and fared sumptuously every day:

And there was a certain beggar named Lazarus, which was laid at his gate, full of sores, and desiring to be fed with the crumbs which fell from the rich man's table, moreover the dog's came and licked his sores.
And it came to pass that the beggar died, and was carried by the angels into Abraham's bosom: the rich man also died, and was buried;

And in hell he lifted up his eyes, being in torments he seeth Abraham afar off, and Lazarus in his bosom.

And he cried and said, "Father of Abraham, have mercy on me, and send Lazarus, that he may dip, the tip of his finger in water, to cool my tongue; for I am tormented in this (fire) flame."

But Abraham said, "Son remember that thou in thy lifetime receivest thy good things, and likewise Lazarus evil things: but now he is comforted and thou art tormented.

And beside all this, between us and you there is a great gulf fixed: so that they which would pass from hence to you cannot; neither can they pass to us that would come from thence."

Then he said, "I pray thee therefore, father, that thou wouldest send him to my father's house:
For I have five brethren; that he may testify unto them, lest they also come into this place of torment."

Abraham saith unto him, "They have Moses and the prophets; let them hear them."

And he said, "Nay, father Abraham: but if one went unto them from the dead, they would repent."

And he said unto him, "If they hear not Moses and the prophets, neither will they be persuaded, thou one rose from the dead."

There is a choice to be made; I earnestly BESEECH (Beg) you that you choose life.
AMEN.

For there is hope of a tree, if it be cut down, that it will sprout again. and that the tender branch thereof will not cease.
Though the root thereof wax old in the earth, and the stock thereof die in the ground,

Yet through the scent of water it will bud and bring forth broughts like a plant.

As the valleys are spread forth, as Lign Aloes (Agallocha) which the Lord hath planted and as cedar trees beside the waters he shall pour the water out of his bucket, and his seed shall be in many waters. (He's talking about the flood in Noah's day. This seed will never be destroyed or lose it's power or come to destruction: no matter how extreme the conditions are.)

Thus were the visions of my head, in my bed; I saw, and behold a tree in the midst of the earth, and the height thereof was great, whose leaf did not fade neither was the fruit thereof destroyed. it brought forth new fruit according to his months, because their waters they issued out of the sanctuary: and the fruit thereof was for meat and the leaf thereof was for medicine.

Jesus is still saying, "He that hath an ear what the Spirit saith unto the churches: to him that overcometh will I give to eat of the tree of life (Agallocha), which is in the midst of the paradise of God."

THE END

P.S. I want to continue to see you in life.

This book was inspired from God through the Holy Spirit, for such a time as this.

I was in deep prayer for my Pastor, and was led to the book of Genesis. There I began to read the second through the third chapter.

When I begin to read about the tree of life that was protected by flaming swords and an angel to keep Adam and Eve from it; I was just taken that through the flood and every thing being destroyed, "Could this tree make it until now?" Or was it destroyed in the flood?"

That is when I asked God the question, not really expecting an answer, But I heard yes, a soft yes. So I asked what is the name of the tree? And I heard one word: AGALLOCHA.

Warnette B. Patterson

Now I know why God put a flaming sword about the tree that turned every way to keep the way of the tree of life.

I invite you to read and see that the tree still exists and is well today.

AGALLOCHA, a truth told from God's own account of how he has preserved this tree. Follow the WORD from GENESIS to REVELATIONS.

AGALLOCHA, THE TREE OF LIFE, MADE ALIVE, ETERNITY